MONTREAL'S OTHER MUSEUMS

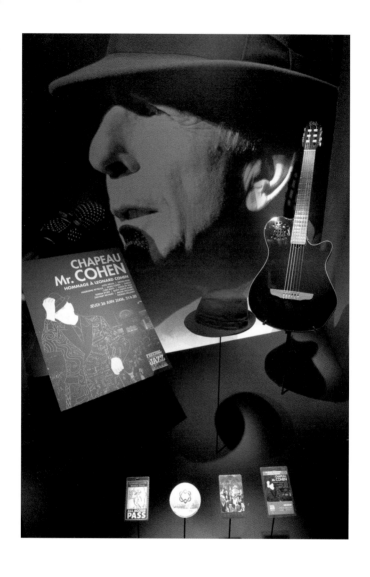

Leonard Cohen display at the Bell Legends of the
Festival Museum.

Montreal's Other Museums

OFF THE BEATEN TRACK

Rachelle Alkallay

Véhicule Press

Published with the assistance of the Canada Book Fund of the
Department of Canadian Heritage.

Cover design: David Drummond
Author photo: Chirag Pandya
Typeset in Minion and Filosofia by Simon Garamond
Printed by Marquis Printing Inc.

LIBRARY AND ARCHIVES CANADA CATALOGUING IN PUBLICATION

Alkallay, Rachel, author
Montreal's other museums : off the beaten track / Rachelle
Alkallay.

Includes index.
ISBN 978-1-55065-354-0 (pbk.)

1. Museums—Québec (Province)—Montréal—Guidebooks.
2. Montréal
(Québec)—Guidebooks. I. Title.

AM22.M65A45 2013   069.09714'27   C2013-902821-8

Published by Véhicule Press, Montréal, Québec, Canada
www.vehiculepress.com

Distribution in Canada by LitDistCo
www.litdistco.ca

Distributed in the U.S. by Independent Publishers Group
www.ipgbook.com

Printed in Canada on FSC certified paper

MUSEUM

a. a building used for storing; preserving, and exhibiting objects considered to be of lasting historical, scientific, or cultural interest.

The Canadian Oxford Paperback Dictionary, 2000

Contents

Note

Montreal is a bilingual French city; most museum displays are in French and English unless otherwise noted. Where tours are offered, specify if you want an English tour to assure its availability.

Many of Montreal's offbeat museums are small and run by volunteers; some are located in universities, schools, and other institutions. Days and opening hours can and do change from season to season and year to year, and museum websites can be out-of-date. Hours and fees are accurate as of press time, but call or e-mail first to be sure the doors will be open for you to feast on their delights.

Enjoy your museum quest!

Preface

The idea for *Montreal's Other Museums* came from a simple question: How many museums do you think there are in Montreal? I guessed around fifty. When the actual jaw-dropping number was revealed*, I was off and running to discover these hidden gems, often unknown to but a handful of volunteers and aficionados.

The journey was as fascinating as the actual visits. Several people had fond memories of the Midget's Palace which closed in the early 1970s; others had heard of a doll museum in Old Montreal (also closed); a friend and I chased down a museum of protest against the City of Westmount in a decrepit building in St-Henri (temporarily closed). The museum dedicated to the great Maurice "the Rocket" Richard had been disbanded; likewise the museum at Notre-Dame Basilica. The Grévin Museum of celebrity wax figures opened as I was finishing *Montreal's Other Museums*. I'm still searching for the rumoured button museum.

Some of these museums go by other names: mediathèque, historical association, heritage centre, and econo-museum, but they all fit the criteria of preservation, storage, and display of objects. They are housed above shops, hidden in industrial buildings, stuffed in converted barns, or secreted on the upper floors of organizational edifices. Most are not obvious at street level. Many are run by dedicated volunteers with a passion for their subject. One curator told me, "I'm having so much fun I can't believe I'm getting paid."

Most of Montreal's offbeat museums have little or no budget, and depend on donations to keep going. Museum collections have been gathered over a period of years; the majority have been donated, tracked down, amassed over the decades, discovered in an aunt's attic, or unearthed at garage sales. The people running them live and breathe the subject, waxing poetic when describing the displays.

Many thanks to Simon Dardick of Véhicule Press for having the faith in me to do this project, and to Vicki Marcok for her practical suggestions and for listening to a writer's woes. A huge thank-you goes to Joan O'Malley for asking the original question that sent me on this fascinating museum quest. To Simcha, Danielle, Pnina, Darinel, Karina, Francesca, Rhona, Estelle, Angela, Terry, Tova, and the rest of my friends at Chabad Queen Mary, who encouraged me and promised to visit all these museums. To Reevin Pearl for creative ways of looking at museum buildings. To Joey Kary for adventures in finding museums. To Roselyne Cazazian, Renee Katz, Kamini Dass, Vivian Tawil, Kim Williams, Alan Hochstein, and the late Michael Shaffer, Z"L, for the late-night phone calls. To fellow writers Joel Yanofsky for tips on unblocking writer's block and Glen Rotchin for great discussions on the art of writing. To my mother, Tova Alkallay, for her unwavering belief in me and for her eternal optimism, and to my father, the late Isaac Alkallay, Z'L, who would have loved to visit all the military and telecommunications museums with me, had he known they existed. This book's for you, Abba.

*How many museums are there in Montreal?
Over 200, and counting ...

The Anna McPherson Collection is a fascinating retrospective on how scientists worked in the not too distant past.

Anna McPherson Collection

Two hundred years ago, scientific instruments were not the sleek computer-based objects found in today's physics labs. They were clunky, metallic, and were manually operated.

The Anna McPherson Collection at McGill University, curated by Professor Emeritus Jean Barrette, who also curates the Ernest Rutherford Museum next door, provides a fascinating retrospective on how scientists worked in the not too distant past. Anna McPherson was one of the very few women who graduated in physics and mathematics at McGill in the 1920s. She received her Ph.D at the University of Chicago in 1933, but couldn't stay away from her alma mater, becoming a demonstrator and instructor in Radio Mechanics during the 1940s. She retired as an associate professor in 1970, and with one foot still in the lab, continued as an honorary visiting professor until her death in 1979.

Optics was her specialty, and optical instruments, preserved by McPherson, polished to perfection, continue to fascinate in their wooden cabinets. The instruments give the non-scientist pause for thought. What is a Kelvin current balance? What do electrostatic chimes do? An iron-tuning fork? And a Marconi wireless detector? Professor Barrette has the answers. He knows each instrument and its function, and is more than happy to give a brief education on each—in French or English.

A couple of the prized objects in the collection are a copy of Newton's *Opticks*, the germinal work on physics, dated 1704, and the first X-ray of a human. Connecting the McPherson Collection to the Rutherford Museum (see p. 79) is Sir Ernest's personal desk, the twin to the one next door.

McGill University, Rutherford Physics Building,
3600 University, Room 111
514.398.7030   www.physics.mcgill.ca/museum/macpherson_collection.htm
Métro/Bus: McGill; Bus 24
Hours: Mon.-Fri. by appointment only; closed during
   Christmas holidays
Tours: yes, by reservation only | Fee: free | Gift shop: no
Cafeteria: no | |Wheelchair access: partial

Religious objects crafted in silver create an impressive display
at the Aron Museum.

Aron Museum

At the Aron Museum at Temple Emanu-El-Beth Shalom most objects on display are directly related to Judaism and the diaspora of the Jewish people. Artifacts from Uzbekistan, Hungary and Russia vie for space with objects from Israel, the Netherlands, and Turkey. The collection of mostly silver objects had its modest start with five pieces donated in 1953 by Anna and Josef Aron of Germany. The Temple's renowned Rabbi Harry Stern suggested that the pieces form the foundation for a museum.

The gleaming glass walls of the museum are a perfect entree into its collection. A perfume bottle from the second century CE, and cosmetic glass from the third century CE Middle East, a Damascene charity box in brass, silver and gold, a terracotta Canaanite cup from 1400 BCE, a turquoise-studded musical clock, delicately worked in gilded bronze, all give voice to artistic creativity over the millennia.

One exhibit displays money from the Theresienstadt "show" camp in Czechoslovakia, used by the Nazis to demonstrate to the world how "normal" life was for inmates, many of whom were children. An azure chuppah (wedding canopy) from a D.P. camp, with silk fringes made in Israel, was used by many couples who married beneath it. The marriages, many of which took place in the shadows of the death camps, demonstrated the optimism of a people facing the future despite the loss of family, home, and country. They placed mezzuzahs on the doorways of their modest homes, though they likely were not the Chagall and Lalique ones in the collection.

Thanks to a modest acquisition, assisted with donations from members, the Aron Museum keeps adding to one of the most important Judaica collections in Canada.

Museum entrance at 395 Elm Street, Westmount
514.937.3575, ext. 230 www.templemontreal.ca/about-us/museum-and-gallery
Métro/Bus: Atwater; Bus 24 or 138
Hours: Friday evenings, 7:45-8:15 p.m. or by appointment; closed all Jewish holidays
Tours: yes (by appointment) | Fee: free | Gift shop: upstairs
Cafeteria: no | Wheelchair access: yes

Painting by Deborah Wright of the façade of the Avmor building, Old Montreal.

Avmor Collection

How many ways can a building be depicted artistically? According to the Avmor Collection on Ste-Hélène Street—at least four hundred ways, and counting.

The genesis of this eccentric art collection housed in the original headquarters of the Avmor specialty cleaning products company occurred in 1965, when businessman Avi Morrow—now a sprightly man in his eighties—commissioned Canadian artist R.D. Wilson to create a painting of the building. From that stately first pen and ink drawing various artistic renditions of the 1861 building snowballed, eventually taking over all the walls of the first floor.

The elegant grey building in the heart of Old Montreal is depicted in painting, sculpture, decorative plates, stained glass, and photography. Some paintings focus on the architecturally impressive front door, while the blue Avmor awning is the centrepiece of attention in others. A roulette wheel decorated with 445 puzzle pieces is yet another original view. A painted tie hangs insouciantly over another work.

The Junk Collection on the third floor is comprised of the stuff people can't bear to throw out. Friends tossed their bits and bobs to Morrow, who framed the items as collages on painted backgrounds. Thus, one person's junk drawer reveals costume jewelry and hair combs; another, keys and rusted metal objects; a third, sports decals and key chains.

Down a floor is the Millennium Collection—paintings created in anticipation of the year 2000, as well as tastefully displayed artifacts: old typewriters, sewing machines, a baby pram, and a camera, and other everyday objects of the past century.

445 Ste-Hélène, Old Montréal
514.282.3301   www.avmor.com/collection.php
Métro/Bus: Square-Victoria
Hours: by appointment only | Tours: yes | Fee: free
Gift shop: no | Cafeteria: no | Wheelchair access: no

(top) Painting of the Bank of Montreal's orginal building in Old Montreal, 1817.
(bottom) The Bank of the People amalgamated with the Bank of Montreal in 1840.

Bank of Montreal Museum

Remember the old joke "Do you have two fives for a ten?" "No, but I can change you two fours for an eight"? In 1840 you could, when banks printed their own money. As displayed at the Bank of Montreal Museum located at the bank's head office in the heart of Old Montreal, what would be considered "funny money" today was "good money" yesteryear.

Canada's first bank, the Bank of Montreal, opened its doors on St-Paul Street in Old Montreal in 1817, and introduced order to the previously chaotic paper-money-and-barter system of financial dealings. Bills were imaginatively decorated with Greek and Roman gods and goddesses and Amerindian chiefs, before Queen Victoria made an appearance. Coins were weighed on scales to make certain that no "clipping" took place. A display of paper notes with obvious errors show that counterfeiting is a time-honoured tradition. And money was transported for security in the heavy Miller chest located at the museum entrance. Dioramas and photographs depict the bank's role in Canadian history: financing the first telegraph line, the railroad system, the Lachine Canal, and its first banks—a clapboard A-frame in Regina, a barbershop in B.C.

As well, the bank considered it a responsibility to teach children the importance of saving money. Hence the delightful 1880s mechanical savings banks in the form of Punch and Judy and Jonah and the Whale, and the concept of saving pennies for a rainy day. Children enjoyed saving money using bankbooks illustrated with nursery rhyme characters. Memorial Books at the front of the museum sombrely honour the bank's employees who lost their lives in the world wars.

129 St-Jacques, Old Montreal
514.877.6810 | e-mail: yolaine.toussaint@bmo.com
Métro/Bus: Place-d'Armes, then bus 55
Hours: Mon.–Fri., 10 a.m.–4 p.m.; closed statutory holidays
Tours: self-guided only | Fee: free
Gift shop: no | Cafeteria: no | Wheelchair access: yes

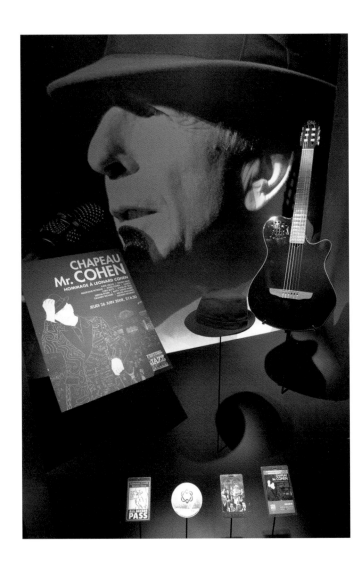

Leonard Cohen display at the Bell Legends of the Festival Museum.

Bell Exhibtion of the
Legends of the Festival Museum

From a clothing emporium to the heart of the renowned Montreal Jazz Festival, it's been quite a journey for the elegant Blumenthal Building at the corner of Ste-Catherine and Bleury streets. Although it had fallen into disrepair, the seven-storey structure built in 1911 was considered a prime example of Canadian commercial architecture. Restored and renamed the *Maison du Festival Rio Tinto Alcan*, the building contains the l'Astral jazz club, a boutique chock full with Yves Archambault's stylized cool St-Cat—symbol of the Montreal Jazz Festival—and the Balmoral restaurant and terrasse overlooking the Quartier des Spectacles, where much of the jazz happens.

The Bell Exhibition of the Legends of the Festival Museum, on the second floor, is a coolly black space streaked with purple and gold lighting where Leonard Cohen sings "Hallelujah" and Diana Krall's cool voice sets its own unrivalled standard. Montreal's own Oscar Peterson's piano and dinner jacket are displayed next to Buddy Guy's black-and-white polka dotted guitar. Charlie Biddle's double bass holds court next to records by Vic Vogel's Big Band, Montreal's Oliver Jones, and Guy Nadon's home-made drum kit.

You can groove to the sounds of the biggest jazz festival in the world (Guinness World Record in 2004, with 1,913,868 visitors) as the back wall comes alive with past concerts performed by the legendary Stevie Wonder and by the First Lady of Song, Ella Fitzgerald. "Yeah!," you agree as you pick up the headphones and move to the beat of All That Jazz...

Maison du Festival Rio Tinto Alcan
305 Ste-Catherine Street W., 2nd floor
Tel.: 514.288.8882 | www.montrealjazzfest.com
Métro/Bus: Place-des-Arts; bus 80 or 15
Hours: Tues.-Wed., 11:30-6 p.m.; Thurs.-Sat., 11:30-9 p.m.; Sun: 11:30-5 p.m.; closed Mon.; longer hours during the Jazz Festival
Tours: self-guided | Fee: free | Gift shop: Boutique downstairs
Cafeteria: Balmoral Restaurant | Wheelchair access: yes

A preserved speciman of Aralia nudicaulis or wild sarsaparilla,
in the Biodiversity Centre's collection.

Biodiversity Centre

Université de Montreal's interactive glass-enclosed Biodiversity Centre, located at the Montreal Botanical Gardens, contains many fascinating aspects of the natural world. Located on one of the floors above is the Ouellet-Robert Entomology Collection. The pristine-looking laboratory, a collector's dream, is named after two Québec priests, Father Ouellet and Father Robert, who collected enormous numbers of specimens.

In the skillful hands of entomologist Dr. Louise Cloutier, bugs and other creepy-crawlies of the multi-footed variety become fascinating creatures with individual characteristics and species' history. Stored away in sliding white cabinets, nearly 50,000 specimens, of 1.5 million species worldwide, have been catalogued. On another floor, the second largest university herbarium in Canada thrives with a collection begun by Brother Marie-Victorin, founder of the Botanical Gardens and the herbarium that bears his name. His name is still spoken with reverence, seventy years after his passing.

Collection coordinator Geoffrey Hall leads hundreds of students annually through the storage cabinets that make up the Herbarium. Students have a chance to see volunteers carefully doing the delicate, and sometimes tedious, work of removing pressed plants from the books, placing them under a microscope, and putting a name to them.

Of the estimated 280,000 species of plants worldwide, Canada is home to 6,000. Thus far, the collection has identified 50,000 plants; more than 200,000 remain to be identified. At Marie-Victorin, many donations of private collections have added enormously to their numbers of plants. The 150 notebooks of Pierre Dansereau, who collected plants worldwide but particularly in the tropics, are housed and used at the Herbarium; as are the meticulous notes of Brother Marie-Victorin, in spidery, still legible ink.

A mushroom collection is the largest in Québec; a peek through the glass windows affords a look at giant specimens with spotted caps, and smaller ones wearing workaday brown caps.

(top) The Biodiversity Centre located on the grounds of Montreal's Botanical Gardens.
(bottom) A sample of the Centre's collection of insects.

PLEASE NOTE:
There is an admission fee to enter the Botanical Gardens.

4101 Sherbrooke Street East, entrance through the Botanical Gardens Greenhouse
Biodiversity Centre: 514.343.2066
Métro/Bus: Pie-IX; Bus 139
Fee: free for the Centre and the Collections
Gift shop: in the greenhouse building
Cafeteria: on the grounds
Wheelchair access: yes to the Centre; partial access to the Collections

Tours (30 minutes) on Wednesday at 2 p.m. (French); ask regarding English tours
Website: www.irbv.umontreal.ca

THE COLLECTIONS

Ouellet-Robert Collection: **514.343.6111**, ext. 82703
Tours: (individual or small groups) by reservation only
Website: www.irbv.umontreal.ca/recherche/collections/collection-entomologique-ouellet-robert

Marie-Victorin Herbarium: 514.343.6111, ext. 82095
Tours: (individual or small groups) Wed.: 2 p.m., by reservation only
Website: www.irbv.umontreal.ca/recherche/collections/herbier-marie-victorin

This display depicts the history of the Black Watch, and soldiers in regimental regalia.

Black Watch (RHR) of Canada Museum

Like a dignified castle, the armoury stands proudly at the corner of Bleury and President Kennedy. Built circa 1905, it became the home of the Black Watch Royal Highland Regiment of Canada, the oldest Scottish highland regiment in Canada. The volunteer regiment originally drew its men from Montreal's Scottish elite including the Birks, Molson, and Ogilvy families. The Regiment contributed 11,000 officers and members to World War I, 2,000 of whom fell in action, many at the Battle of Vimy Ridge.

By 1970, the Black Watch had evolved into a regular battalion serving in the Canadian Army, and has continued to serve in every war since, including Afghanistan.

Kilts, bearskin hat and flaming red feathers, are some of the unique items on display at the museum on the ground floor of the armoury. A sombre reminder of the costs of war, the recently renovated museum is also a joyful celebration of proud, ancient traditions.

Guns and rifles, drums and bugles, field maps, and medals carefully laid out against a red velvet background give vibrancy to the Regiment's life in war and in peace. The Royal Stuart tartan, used by the pipers of the Black Watch, adds a touch of colour to the wood-panelled museum.

A life-size portrait of the first Canadian to receive the Victoria Cross, youthful Lance-Corporal Frederick Fisher of Westmount, killed in action in World War I, is mounted near King George V's personal condolence letter to his parents. A thank-you note with violets, from the late Scottish-born Queen Mother Elizabeth, who was Colonel-in-Chief of the Regiment, adds a special touch (Prince Charles now holds that title).

2067 Bleury Avenue
514.496.1686, x 230 www.blackwatchcanada.com/en/
heritage-and-history/museum-and-archives
Métro/Bus: Place-des-Arts; Bus 15, 80
Hours: Tuesdays; hours vary from season to season
Tours: yes; call for appointment
Fee: free | Gift shop: display case | Cafeteria: no
Wheelchair access: yes

(top) The Fairchild FC-2 Razorback aircraft was one of the first bush planes to have a heated cabin, equipped with a camera in the rear fuselage which was used to take aerial pictures.

(bottom) Located on the ground floor, the Godfrey Stewart Pasmore Aviation Art Gallery houses some of the best aviation paintings that represent historical moments in Québec aviation.

Canadian Aviation Heritage Centre

The Canadian Aviation Heritage Centre, housed in an old stone barn on the West Island, is home to a number of aircraft such as a World War II Bolingbroke, a Blériot XI, a FC-2 Razorback, and 7,500 books on aviation. Montreal and its surroundings are home to a major aerospace industry and the city's involvement with aviation took off with the flight of *Le Scarabée*, a Blériot IX flown by Count Jacques de Lesseps on July 2, 1910 from Pointe-Claire. It is being painstakingly reproduced by a team of dedocated volunteers, using Douglas fir for its wings and white ash for the body.

The Gordon Stewart Pasmore Gallery on the ground floor houses some of the best aviation paintings in Canada, including many done by Pasmore. Pasmore is the rescuer of the Old Stone Barn, which was derelict and ready for demolition, before he obtained a lease from McGill University, turning it into this centre celebrating Canadian aviation with a focus on Québec.

On the first floor black-and-white photographs of World War II planes come to life in the form of the Fairchild Bolingbroke Mk IV, a coastal patrol plane made in Longueuil by Fairchild Aircraft where over 600 were produced; the model here is one of them, and it has taken volunteers six years just to finish the nose section. Where parts no longer exist, they are fabricated at the Aviation Centre. Patrick Campbell, a retired engineer and World War II veteran, is the lead on the latest project—a Curtis-Reid Rambler, designed and built in Montreal. Other objects of past eras line the walls of the enormous former barn—an old Philips radio, a course-setting bombsight, a free-standing pilot seat, receivers, and numerous displays.

McGill University, Macdonald Campus,
21111 Lakeshore Blvd., Ste-Anne-de-Bellevue
514.398.7948 www.cahc-ccpa.com
Métro/Bus: Bus 211, 419 (weekdays only)
Hours: Mon./Tues./Sat., 9:30 a.m.–2:30 p.m.
Tours: yes; call for appointment
Fee: suggested donation of $5 | Gift shop: display case
Cafeteria: no | Wheelchair access: ground floor only

(top) The coat of arms of the Canadian Forces Logistics branch.
(bottom) Retired WWII machine guns encased behind glass.

Canadian Forces Logistics Museum

The art of folding a parachute is a specialized skill performed by trained riggers. Any paratrooper who depends on the billowing folds of silk to unravel in precisely the right way when hurtling to earth at 100+ mph would agree.

Dr. Andrew Gregory, who runs the museum, explains that a soldier's vest— 22 lbs *without* any added gear—needs strength and endurance. Logistics is army-speak for the division that takes care of all supplies for the Armed Forces: food, ammunition, transport. Of 60,000 members of the Armed Forces, 13,000 are "loggies", men and women trained as soldiers, holding jobs with the same risks as other members of the Forces. They are out in the field, coordinating the thousands of items that make the Canadian Armed Forces run smoothly.

Dr. Gregory enjoys teaching museum visitors the place of logistics within Canadian military history. Canada learned to be supply independent during the Korean War; before that, it relied on its allies to move around its supplies.

Unexpected oddities can be seen—Prussian war helmets, a set of precisely laid-out crystal glasses, a scale model of an oil replenishment vessel, a painting of the Queen wearing a 108-diamond brooch presented to her in 1959 at the opening of the St. Lawrence Seaway, which she returned in 2000.

The museum is currently being revamped, but remains open to the public. The museum is surrounded by the largest military vehicle yard in Québec. Look for the tanks on the lawn and you will know you have arrived.

6560 Hochelaga Street (beside entrance to the Longue-Pointe Garrison)
514.252.2777 x 2241 http://cflogmuseum.ca
Métro/Bus: Pie-IX métro, then bus 85 East; or, Langélier métro, then bus 85 west
Hours: Wed.-Sun., 10 a.m.- 4 p.m.; closed Mon., Tues., and statutory holidays
Tours: yes; groups up to 30 with reservations | Fee: donation
Gift shop: display case | Cafeteria: no | Wheelchair access: yes (via the rear door)

The façade of the Centre of Contemporary Arts of Québec,
formerly a fire station.

Centre of Contemporary Arts of Québec

Museums and our concept of them is changing. Today, museums do more than preserve and exhibit objects; often they participate actively in the creation of art.

The red-painted doors of the Centre of Contemporary Arts of Québec presents one of these changing faces. Opened in 1993, it is housed in a converted fire station on St-Dominique Street in the Plateau district. Inside is a bright white space with twenty-foot high ceilings, a perfect blank canvas on which artists create works of sculpture, display works of photography, and present experimental theatre. Upstairs, overlooking the exhibition space, surrounded by paintings and binders of previous shows, is the energetic director Dominique Rolland, who created the outdoor sculpture museum along the Lachine Canal. Rolland explains that the centre, which receives no government grants, is therefore "free as the wind" to experiment and create, a completely organic space. It is the only centre of its kind in Canada.

In the atélier, artist-in-residence Marc Lincourt works on small papier-maché castings of a tour de force—his alphabet project portraying its origins in Mesopotamia to the present day. Within each letter is the history of the letter, capturing the origin of writing and the artistry of each letter. When the project is completed, it will occupy an estimated 350 feet in a sculpture garden where the giant letters will be seen from above.Visitors will wander inside the alphabet, experiencing the birth of writing.

Exhibits change every two months; live performances, discussions, and conferences are interspersed with the exhibitions.

4247 St-Dominique, Plateau district
514.842.4300
Métro/Bus: St-Laurent, then bus 55
Hours: Mon.-Fri., 10 a.m.- 5 p.m.; reservations preferred
Tours: by reservation | Fee: free; events vary in price
Gift shop: no | Cafeteria: no | Wheelchair access: yes
Website: no

A barn owl contemplates his surroundings at the Eco-Museum Zoo.

Eco-Museum Zoo

The luxuriant white-furred Arctic fox lies in one of the first enclosures at Ste-Anne-de-Bellevue's Eco-Museum Zoo, a living museum of native Québec species where you can discover the playfulness of the northern river otter along with the peculiar charm of the turkey vulture.

Long winding paths are carved out from the marshlands, precursors of the zoo prior to its founding in 1981 by the St. Lawrence Valley Natural History Society. This is a slice of real Canadian woodlands; the animals are relaxed and unafraid. Ravens perch silently inside their aviary, watching, observing. Their cousins in the next aviary, the crows, are a contrast in character as they keep up a constant commentary.

The Light into Dark exhibit in the main building is lined with aquariums of painted turtles, croaking bug-eyed bullfrogs, and the appropriately-named largemouth bass. Think Harry Potter and the hissing snake who speaks to him, and you'll appreciate the milk snake slithering silently on branches, tongue flickering.

Frog Call Nights and Animal Care Apprentice days for budding zoologists continue the ideas of Dr. Roger Bider, founder of the Society, whose aim was to teach animal and nature appreciation to children. Adults can also participate in Breakfast with the Animals and Twilight at the Zoo events, which take place beyond regular Eco-Museum hours and where creatures of the night greet you.

21125 chemin Ste-Marie, Ste-Anne-de-Bellevue
514.457.9449 | www.ecomuseum.ca
Métro/Bus: 211, 419 (weekdays only)
Hours: 9:00 a.m.-5:00 p.m.; closed Christmas Day
Tours: Self-guided; special activities for groups of 20 or more
    by reservation
Fee: Adults: $15; Seniors: $12; Children (3 to 15): $9;
    Toddlers (2 and under): free
Gift shop: yes | Cafeteria: vending machines |
Wheelchair access: partial

In the workshop, the seamstress meticulously brings together the various pieces of a garment to create unique fur coats and accessories for the shop and the made-to-measure department.

Econo-museum Harricana

Look up, and fur coats of mink, fox, and otter drip luxuriously from the ceilings, keeping company with delicate white silk wedding gowns. Beaver, raccoon, and coyote coats festoon the walls, waiting for restyling as outer garments, hats, purses, earmuffs and jewelry. Nothing is wasted to create Mariouche Gagné's ecoluxe Harricana label,which she founded in 1994. The econo-museum began a few months later.

Gagné grew up near a reserve by the longest river in Québec, the Harricana. Originally anti-fur and preferring to work with faux fur, Gagné discovered that faux fur relies heavily on petrochemicals, lasts only a couple of seasons, and doesn't bio-degrade. The furs used at Harricana come from people selling their vintage furs, sorting plants, and remnants from other furriers.

Operating since 2011 from a refurbished bank, the atelier is ensconced in the former Chubb bank vault holding mannequins sporting recycled fur pieces. The basement now houses the econo-museum. Photographs detail the history of haute couture and its roots in Québec, including designer Michel Robichaud's uniform created for Expo '67 which sold worldwide. Because fashion and good fabrics were an ocean and months away, Québec dressmakers used creativity to look stylish. During World War II, the government took out ads to show women how to recycle old furs and clothing. Recycling fur into new fashions has saved the lives of thousands of furry creatures over the past twenty years it also stretches out the life of garments for decades.

An otter in the wild is thankful!

3000 St-Antoine Street West
514.287.6517, ext. 200   www.harricana.qc.ca
Métro/Bus: Lionel-Groulx
Hours: Mon.-Fri., 10 a.m.-4 p.m.; on weekends for groups by reservation
Tours: by reservation only; groups up to 15 people
Fee: $5 (subject to change); fee refunded upon any purchase
Gift shop: yes | Cafeteria: no | Wheelchair access: partial

Distant relatives of the violin include the Arab rebab and the viola.

Econo-museum of the Violin

What are violins made of? Curly maple. All violins. Always. And nearly always from the forests of Germany.

And what is the soul of the violin? A small 10 mm dowel made of spruce placed between the top-plate and the back-plate of a violin and held together by its perfect placement, not with glue. A violin is a small individually hand-carved masterpiece; violin bow-making is a separate craft.

These are some of the delightful secrets of violins divulged on a tour of the Econo-museum of the Violin, a charming place that combines interpretation of artifacts on display, research, and a production workshop, as part of the econo-museum concept that originated in Québec.

The museum is the creation of Jules Saint-Michel (originally Gyula Szentmihalyí), a transplanted Hungarian who brought the beauty of violins with him when he fled the Hungarian Revolution in 1956 and arrived in Montréal, via a detour to Paris where he met his Québécoise wife, in the late 1950s. His dream to create a museum above his violin shop came to fruition in 1999. The master's hands were depicted on a 10-cent Canadian stamp celebrating musicians in 1998.

The violins and their stringed relatives are displayed against rich red velvet. A form of the violin appears in Arab culture as the rebab; the Chinese and the Ceylonese also played stringed instruments. The father of the modern violin is considered to be the Cremonese luthier Andrea Amati. His sons and grandsons followed in the profession, and taught Stradivarius and Guarneri. Copies of Stradivarius's and Amati's instruments, and the original violin from the film, *The Red Violin*, shot in Montreal in 1998, form part of the unique display at the Econo-museum.

57 Ontario Street West
514.288.4343 www.luthiersaintmichel.com
Métro: Place-des-Arts, then bus 80
Hours: Tues./Thurs. 2 p.m.–5 p.m.
Tours: yes, in French and English; reservations required
Fee: $8 | Gift shop: yes | Cafeteria: no | Wheelchair access: partial

A crown-topped torah in its embroidered cover.

Edward Bronfman Museum, Congregation Shaar Hashomayim

Polished silver glimmers magnificently throughout the compact, softly-lit museum at the Shaar Hashomayim, Montreal's oldest Ashkenazi synagogue. Full of historical objects that speak of the Jewish people's diaspora, the museum opens with a pair of wood benches used in the late 19th century at the English, German and Polish Synagogue on McGill College Avenue. A "Welcome to our table" set with white china, lettered in gold with CSH and matching heavy silverware, gives visitors a taste of the synagogue's elegance. Two enormous, ornate Shabbat candelabra donated by Milly Lande, member of the prominent Bronfman family, to the now-closed Montefiore Club, link the objects with the chronicle of the Jewish community. The museum is named after Milly Lande's cousin, the philanthropist and businessman Edward Bronfman.

The words of Rabbi Abraham Joshua Heschel, "Just to be is a blessing. . . just to live is holy" are inscribed on an elaborate cloth wall runner. Holy objects, such as a 16th-century *Ner Tamid* (Eternal Flame) lamp stolen by the Nazis during World War II and given to the congregation in 2001, speak of the long route some artifacts took to arrive at their destination. Behind glass-fronted display cases many valuable relics are displayed, including eight-branched *Chanukkiot* from Poland, Mandatory Palestine, India, and Germany; Torah pointers from Italy, the Netherlands, and North Africa; a Viennese Torah Ark from 1887 elaborately carved with lions of Judah, menorahs and mythical griffins; and a German hand-lettered Torah binder made to commemorate the birth of Siegfried Guggenheim of the renowned New York family.

450 Kensington Avenue, Westmount
514.937.9471 www.shaarhashomayim.org
Métro/Bus: 24 or 138
Hours: Mon.-Fri., 9 a.m.-5 p.m.; closes early for Shabbat; closed on all Jewish holidays
Tours: no | Fee: free | Gift shop: yes | Cafeteria: no
Wheelchair access: yes

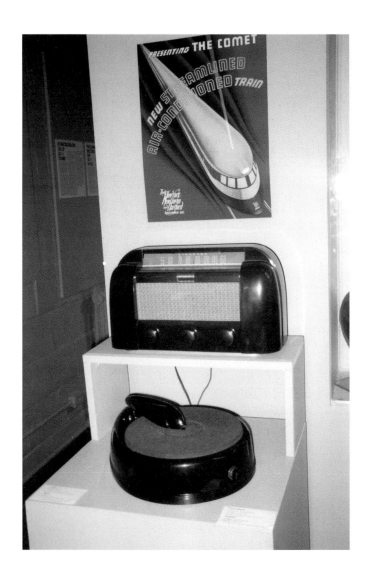

The Emile Berliner Museum is a treasure trove of vintage radios and record players. The turntable pictured here is made of wood, circa 1926.

Emile Berliner Museum

Who invented the gramophone?

Thomas Edison? Wrong. Montreal plays a big part in the early history of electronic sound and recordings, thanks to Emile Berliner, a German-born Jew who came to Canada via the United States at the turn of the 20th century. He invented both the first gramophone and flat records, followed by a method of pressing records. Before these inventions, while living in the United States, Berliner invented the first telephone transmitter microphone used by Alexander Graham Bell, then co-founded a company to produce records.

A huge purple record greets you on the ground floor leading to the Emile Berliner Museum on Lacasse Street, former site of the Berliner Gram-o-phone Company (1908).

This compact, second-floor museum is a treasure trove of early telecommunications equipment made of metal, wood, or steel. Much of it was produced at the now defunct factory that contributed to the industrial boom in working-class St-Henri. The museum is presided over by Nipper the Dog, the RCA-Victor Company mascot. Display terminals make early 20th-century Montreal come alive, as the presence of Berliner's stores and factories, both downtown and in St-Henri, exhibit the influence of the invention of records, victrolas, and recording studios. Black-and-white photographs provide a gritty texture to workers' lives in the Edwardian era and into World War I.

Exhibitions change yearly. The newsletter, *His Master's Voice,* published quarterly by the museum, is available on-site. Day camps for children take place during the summer; call for reservations.

1050 Lacasse Street, C-220
514.932.9663 www.berliner.montreal.museum_
Métro/Bus: St-Henri
Hours: Fri.–Sun., 2 p.m.–5 p.m.; extended summer hours
Tours: self-guided; guides available for large groups by reservation
Fee: $5 suggested donation | Gift shop: no | Cafeteria: no
Wheelchair access: no

The Eudore-Dubeau Museum is a treasure house packed with objects that chronicle the evolution of dentistry.

Eudore-Dubeau Museum

"Owww! That hurts! . . . I'll live with the severe toothache."

That's what yesteryear's dental patient would have said, faced with previous centuries' instruments of dentistry—enormous, menacing sets of clamps, dental forceps, carved ivory instruments, zinc cement—all going into your mouth. . . to make you feel better.

The tools of a dentist's armoury were enough to keep away anyone but the most desperately suffering patient. And for most of dentistry's history, the work was performed without benefit of anesthetic, as the old prints depicting teeth-pulling on unhappy patients at the Eudore-Dubeau Museum at the Université de Montréal demonstrate.

Hidden behind heavy wooden doors, the museum, named after Faculty of Dentistry founder Dr. Eudore Dubeau, is a treasure house packed with objects that chronicle the evolution of oral care: tools used by medieval barbers to extract teeth, a velvet-covered dental chair on a wrought-iron base, and the pedal that made the turbine work to create model teeth.

A floor display shows an elegant Edwardian lady seated in a chair—a porcelain bowl by her side—being watched over by an attentive skeleton, along with comical posters and statuary of dentists. (Who said dentists don't have a sense of humour?)

In a display case, and collected for comparison's sake, animal skulls are exhibited side by side with human skulls, both normally and abnormally shaped. And of course, there are the obligatory boxes of teeth. If you're lucky, André Bérard, who manages the museum and knows every object in the exhibit, will be there at the museum to personalize your tour.

Université de Montréal, Faculty of Dentistry, Pavillon Principal, 2900 Edouard-Montpetit, Porte B-1, Local D-129
514.343.6750 E-mail: musee@medent.umontreal.ca
Métro/Bus: Université de Montréal
Hours: open one day a week and is variable; call for hours
Tours: by reservation | Fee: free | Gift shop: no | Cafeteria: no
Wheelchair access: yes, with difficulty

A group of students admire an exhibition by photographers Isaac and Thomas along the interpretation corridor at the Green Building Discovery Centre.

Green Building Discovery Centre

Hydro-Québec's Green Building Discovery Centre is a model for how future buildings can be designed—a peek into a future where the workplace is healthy, fewer chemicals emanate from building materials, and sick-building syndrome is an illness of the past. It is a place where the ecological footprint is minimal, where sustainable development and social responsibility are the guiding principles. Sidney Ribaux conceived of the Green Building Discovery Centre, where Équiterre now shares space. Inside the building, the air is fresh and pure, with bright green plants climbing a five-storey wall.

Up a staircase made of wood recovered from one-hundred-year-old sunken logs in Georgian Bay, step on a block of ecological Québec-made cement and listen to the guide explain the concept behind the geo-thermal heating and cooling systems.

Panels demonstrate the variety of possibilities of going green in construction. Different types of glass, including recycled broken glass; recycled fibres for carpeting; recycled wood; natural paints: every choice can be a sustainable one in balance with the environment and socially just.

Note that most terminal displays, brochures, and the website are in French only; English tours are available upon request. The Green Building's ecology-related exhibitions—rivers in peril, sustainable lamps, wood creations—change monthly. Conferences and documentaries on sustainable development occur frequently; check the website to participate.

50 Ste-Catherine Street West
514.394.1108 www.lamdd.org
Métro/Bus: Place-des-Arts; Bus 80
Hours: Mon.-Fri., 10:30 a.m.-6 p.m., Sat.-Sun., 10 a.m.-4 p.m.
Tours: Fri., 1:30 p.m. and 5:30 p.m., in French; call for English tours; www.equiterre.org/visits
Fee: free for individuals; charge for groups rleoto@equiterre.org
Giftshop: no | Cafeteria: no | Wheelchair access: yes, by appointment

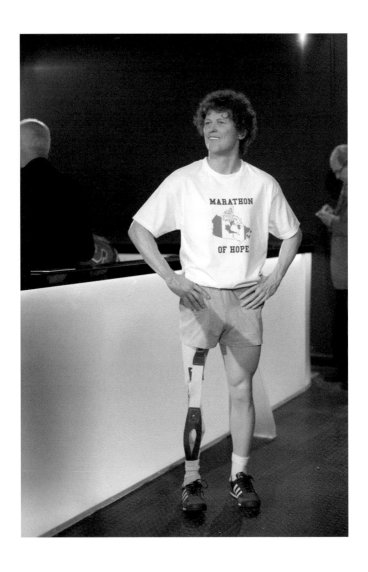

Terry Fox is one of the many personalities populating
the Grévin Wax Museum.

Grévin Wax Museum

From the black corridor with LED lights changing from purple to blue to amber, to the mirrored 3-D presentation of the four seasons complete with fluttering monarch butterflies, the Grévin is a one-of-a-kind wax museum that is experienced through the senses. A tour of the exquisite life-like figures at the red and gold carpeted Grévin Montréal, the first venue outside France for the Paris-based museum, brings you close to Hollywood A-listers like the handsome George Clooney, champagne glass in hand, and Brad Pitt, who stands next to the elegant Meryl Streep. Louis Armstrong trumpets energetically next to an enthusiastic Elton John cavorting at the white baby grand. Other stars pose mincingly at the glittering soirée, as Chef Alain Ducasse casts a discerning eye over the scrumptious pastry-laden dessert table. Quebec's own Ginette Reno smiles in an evening-gown and hockey great Guy Lafleur shares a rink with Sydney Crosby and Mario Lemieux. Onboard a ship, the thoughtful Jacques Cartier sails on a 16th-century voyage across a treacherous Atlantic Ocean. A capsule history of Québec is played out in the exhibition beside him, with Montcalm and Wolfe battling it out in gentlemanly fashion.

The secrets of the Grévin's creations are revealed in the interactive workshop, where assorted heads, torsos, and limbs share space with wigs and theatrical costumes, supervised by Coco Chanel on the stairs of her atelier. In four steps on display screens, a visitor poses for measurements, casting, make-up and costume, and the final result arrives as a CD in the mail.

Eaton Centre, 705 Ste-Catherine St. West, 5th Floor
514.788.5210 www.grevin-montreal.com
Métro/Bus: McGill; Bus 15
Hours: Mon.-Sat.: 10 a.m. - 6 p.m.; Sun.: 11 a.m. - 5 p.m.
Tours: self-guided
Fee: Adults: $17.50; Seniors: $16; Students & children (13 & older): $14; Families: $53; Children 6-12: $12.50
Gift shop: yes | Cafeteria: Europea's Café Grévin
Wheelchair access: yes

(top) The Commodore PET 2001 series, the first all-in-one home computer, was released in June 1977.

(bottom) The rugged-looking Kaypro 4 was released in 1984.

iMusée of Computer History

Take a step back in time—only forty years or so—to appreciate how far, and how fast, computers have evolved from large, clunky desk models to sleek, lightweight laptops and tablets.

Founded in 2008, the iMusée located in Hochelaga-Maisonneuve's Community Education Pavillion—Canada's only permanent museum dedicated to the micro-computer and video games—is the brainchild of Parisian-born Philippe Nieuwbourg. In addition to the museum, he designed the space to be multi-functional to serve the residents of the Hochelaga-Maisonneuve district in Montreal's east end. Space can be booked on one of the computers to work on projects. Children can watch videos and interact with games in an educational way. A professionally-equipped multi-media room for young filmmakers and a video-conference space is available for meetings.

Every computer functions, be it an Apple Lisa from 1983, a 1981 Osborne which demonstrated the possibilities of a portable computer, or a modem with a rotary phone, to demonstrate the importance of remembering the past and the steps it took to bring technology to its present state. An on-site library links the working models and explains concepts such as the DOS operating system.

The display case reveals necklaces and bracelets created from the silvery innards of computers, earrings fashioned from coloured bits of wires, and stylish rings assembled from defunct motherboards. It fits into the museum's philosophy of reusing and recycling all computer bits.

Exhibits change every three to four months.

1691 Pie-IX Blvd.
514.824.6302 www.imusee.org
Métro/Bus: Pie-IX, then bus 139
Hours: Fri.-Sun., 10 a.m.–5 p.m.
Tours: Yes, in English, French, and Spanish; group tours by
    appointment
Fee: $5 donation | Gift shop: display cabinet | Cafeteria: no
Wheelchair access: no

This section of the General Hospital was built in 1693, fifty years after the founding of Montreal, and renovated in 1765.

Maison de Mère d'Youville

In 1765, a fire destroyed part of the General Hospital of Montreal, run by Canada's first saint, Marguerite d'Youville. The blackened wood of the ceiling beams testify to the power of that event, commemorated in a floor-to-ceiling painting on the second floor of La Maison de Mère d'Youville. And today you can still smell the smoke.

The fire did not deter the determined eighteenth-century woman, who was left with two small children after being widowed young following a difficult marriage. Faith born of hardship and vision drove her to found the Sisters of Charity, commonly known as the Grey Nuns, and along with four other women, made it her mission to help the poor and women in difficulty in the young city of Montreal. The giant black cauldrons in several stone-walled rooms on the ground floor testify to the numerous meals fed to the hungry and the indigent. Sister Germaine, the delightful retired nun who gives the English tour, is a font of information on the history of the Old Montreal home, where ten nuns continue to live.

In the Footsteps of Marguerite is an exhibit that celebrates her life in the house in which she lived and performed her charitable acts.

Forks and spoons comprised the silver cutlery service, cedar hand-crafted candlesticks and a working grandfather clock from 1694 were part of Mère d'Youville's surroundings, as were pewter dishes, and wooden salt and pepper shakers carved from apple trees from Chateauguay. An enormous master key served as a passe-partout to all the rooms.

138 St-Pierre, Old Montreal
514.842-9411www.sgm.qc.ca/en/main-nav/saint-marguerite-dyouville
Métro/Bus: Square Victoria
Hours: Tuesday-Sunday, 9:30 a.m.-5 p.m., by reservation
Tours: in French; in English by reservation; max. ten people
Fee: free | Gift shop: yes | Cafeteria: no
Wheelchair accessible: yes

The chairs of the Grand Master of the Masonic
Lodge are quietly impressive.

Masonic Temple Library/Museum

Step into a hidden world—the blue-carpeted Grand Chamber of the Montreal Masonic Memorial Temple, with its carved wooden thrones and hallowed halls to which the secret society allows access. The Grand Chamber radiates serenity. Jacques Ruelland, the volunteer curator and member of the society, explains that the Freemasons are "a society with secrets" —mostly in its initiation rites—rather than a "secret society". Belief in a Supreme Being is an essential qualification to becoming a freemason in this men-only society which includes Christians, Jews, Muslims, and Hindus.

The ornate wooden staircase takes you up to the sixth-floor museum. The square and the compass are symbols of the virtues of work. Silver trowels, symbolizing buildings, are laid out beside a collection of ornate aprons decorated with masonic symbols. The aprons are worn by freemasons and master masons design their own. A triangle, symbolizing the eye of G-d for the ancient Egyptians, has great meaning for masons, and appear on many objects in the museum. Gavels, chisels, and gauges indicate the three different levels of masonry. Tall purple tapers add to the majestic feel of the room. The fez that connects the Freemasons with the Shriners also has a place here, and a collection of pins indicates the international influence of the society.

The Belgian-born Ruelland, a science historian and museologist by training, gathers objects for the museum with the enthusiasm of a born collector. He began putting together the collection in 2007 as a library on freemasonry which currently comprises 4,500 books in a variety of languages.

2295 St-Marc Street
514.933-6739 www.glquebec.org
Métro/Bus: Guy or bus 24 | Hours: by appointment only
Tours: self-guided | Fee: free | Gift shop: no | Cafeteria: no
Wheelchair access: no

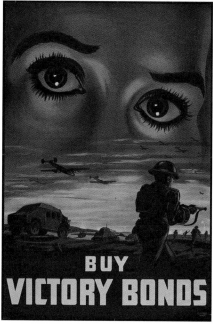

Two items from McGill's Rare Books & Special Collections.
(top) Iroquois who took part in Tercentenary Pageant
(1908), Quebec.
(bottom) Buy Victory Bonds poster. Gordon K. Odell, artist.

McGill University Rare Books & Special Collections

In the anteroom of McGill's Rare Books & Special Collections, delicately traced maps depicting Japan in the days of the shogunate peer out from under glass. In the library, the nineteenth-century *Flora Symbolica*, the *Floral Birthday Book*, and *Common Wayside Flowers*, are the showcase themes. You can see an embroidered cloth map of the world, signed by Frances Levi, Northampton, October 13, 1787.

Busts of America's 16th president, from the Lincoln Collection, decorate much of the library. Access to the Rosalynde Stearn Puppet Collection, the Cookery Book Collection, and the Canadian Olympic Collection is by special request. The collection houses over 500,000 items, including maps, prints, manuscripts, and Bibles in all sizes and languages, with a focus on Canadiana. Ordinary grammar books are quite rare, because "they were used to death," said Dr. Richard Virr, director of Rare Books & Special Collections. Nevertheless, McGill managed to acquire an example of a Donatus Latin Grammar, several hundred years old; it keeps company with three copies of *The Nuremberg Chronicle* of 1493 and an original Latin edition of a work by taxonomist Carl Linnaeus.

While the nature of books is changing, books themselves will always exist, said Dr. Virr. Materials will be used differently in the future, but technology cannot replace the tactile sense of books.

McGill University, McLennan Library Building
3459 MacTavish, 4th floor
514.398.4711
Website: www.mcgill.ca/library/branches/rarebooks
Métro/Bus: McGill; Bus 24
Hours: (summer) Mon.-Fri., 10 a.m.-6 p.m.; closed Dec. 24-
  Jan. 5; May 20; June 24; July 1; Labour Day
Tours: yes, for groups | Fee: free | Gift shop: no
Cafeteria: in the building | Wheelchair access: yes

The entrance to the Médiathèque Jazz/La Presse
on the third floor of the Rio Tinto Alcan Bulding.

Médiathèque Jazz/La Presse

La mémoire est ici. Memory is here, invokes the panel of jazz greats at the entrance of the Médiathèque Jazz/La Presse in the Rio Tinto Alcan building. A cool oasis of jazz knowledge—one of the largest jazz resource centres of its kind in the world—it is located one floor above the Bell Exhibition of the Legends of the Museum of the Festival International de Jazz.

Overlooking the Quartier des Spectacles, the Médiathèque encompasses 50,000 music archives, 30,000 photographs and 1,000 videos and concerts, plus jazz ephemera. Jazz aficionados can tune into their favourite musicians on computer terminals and browse through huge binders of clippings which cover nearly everything written about the world's biggest Jazz Festival.

Montreal jazz journalist Len Dobbin's memorabilia is an important part of the collection. A display case details his notes, radio show, playlists, cassettes, and tape reels acquired by the Médiathèque after he died in 2009.

You can see a copy of the famous photograph, "A Great Day in Harlem, 1958" showing children sitting curbside at the feet of 57 jazz titans. Posters of The Rolling Stones and the original Harlem Shuffle, and the moody drawing of intense jazz enthusiasts, queuing for hours to enter their favourite club in the dark of night, create an atmosphere of cool.

Maison du Festival Rio Tinto Alcan
305 Ste-Catherine Street West, 3rd floor
514.288.8882 www.montrealjazzfest.com/maison-du-festival-online/mediatheque.aspx
Métro/Bus: Place-des-Arts; Bus 80 or 15
Hours: Tues.-Fri. 11:30 a.m.-6 p.m.; closed Sat../Sun./Mon. and Dec. 25-Jan. 3; Jazz Festival hours: daily, 11:30 a.m.-10 p.m.
Tours: self-guided; reservations required for groups
Fee: free | Gift shop: on ground floor | Cafeteria: coffee machine; Balmoral restaurant on ground floor
Wheelchair access: yes

A replica of Gutenberg's printing press dominates the
entrance hall to the Médiathéque Gaëtan-Dostie.

Médiathèque littéraire Gaëtan-Dostie

Actor Gaëtan Dostie, founder of the Médiathèque, chose this historically significant building as the home for his literary collection showcasing North American French literature, with an emphasis on French Québec literature. He began collecting material on printing at the age of nine.

The greystone building with the dark-blue door and French-blue windows was built by businessman Antoine Olivier Berthelet in 1845, in what was then the heart of English Montreal. His mission was, in Dostie's words, to prove that francophones could be financially successful and live an elegant lifestyle.

In 2008, his collection found a home in this heritage building whose interior he worked on for two years before opening it to the public. Every inch of the three-storey building is used to dramatic effect. Each room traces the roots of Quebec's literary tradition decade by decade. Québec's French literature began relatively late, in the latter part of the nineteenth century; the first book written by a woman was published in 1910. Examples of these books are displayed, along with woodblocks, early maps of Montreal, satires, and a stuffed owl sternly overseeing one salon. The Blue Room is dedicated to Émile Nelligan, one of Québec's earliest poets. Posters mark the turbulent 1960s and 1970s when Pierre Vallières and Michèle Lalonde published their works giving voice to pent-up nationalist emotions. A *Dictionnaire de la Censure au Québec*, published in 1977, is a history of literary censorship, mostly by the Church. Only 400 items of the 20,000 artifacts are on exhibit at any time.

More than a museum, the Médiathèque hosts conferences, has a room devoted to printing, and is infused with the love of Québécois literature.

1214 de la Montagne
514.861.0880 www.algi.qc.ca (French only)
Métro/Bus: Peel
Hours: Tues.-Fri., 1 p.m.-5 p.m.
Tours: yes; by reservation | Fee: $10; group rate: $12/person
Gift shop: no | Cafeteria: no | Wheelchair access: partial

The powerful history of the Montreal Canadiens greets the visitor
at the entrance of their Hall of Fame.

Montreal Canadiens Hall of Fame

Hockey stars come alive in living colour at a fascinating interactive display at the Hall of Fame located in the lower reaches of the Bell Centre, where Jean Béliveau answers your questions on his career, Elmer Lach talks about playing a lot of cards on the long train rides between games in the 1940s and Mike Cammalleri tells you why he became interested in a hockey career.

The red, white, and blue of the best hockey team in the NHL (24 Stanley Cups) surrounds you and propels you into the action in a lively museum that promises to make you a fan of the game if you aren't already one. Join the players as they crisscross the continent by train, sleeping in berths on long rides to Chicago and Boston.

Play an interactive hockey game: hear the cheers when you dodge the goalie, shoot and score! Sit on the same red benches as Les Glorieux in a re-creation of the Habs' Forum locker room, and relive the legendary Howie Morenz's 1937 funeral, which drew 15,000 people outside the Forum. Get up close to Rocket Richard's #9 jersey and Jean Beliveau's #4 from 1970-71. Hundreds of cards spanning the decades are displayed on the walls chronologically. And what would hockey be without the legendary rivalries? Enjoy the memorabilia from the Detroit Red Wings, the Toronto Maple Leafs, and the Boston Bruins.

The Canadiens are part of the fabric of Montreal, and the puzzles, posters, patches, pucks, games, and books on the city's favourite team testify to that.

Bell Centre, 1909 Avenue des Canadiens-de-Montréal
514.925.7777 www.hall.canadiens.com
Métro/Bus: Lucien-L'Allier
Hours: Tues.-Sat., 10 a.m.-6 p.m.; Sun., 12:00-5 p.m.; closed Mon.
Tours: only with Bell Centre tour; different price structure
Fee: Adults (17+): $11; Seniors & youth 5-16: $8; Families: $34;
Children under 4: free; $2 less for groups of 20+ with reservations or on game day with tickets
Gift shop: yes | Cafeteria: in the Bell Centre
Wheelchair access: yes

The firefighters museum, which shares this beautiful building with fire station 30, has it's entrance on St-Laurent Boulevard.

Montreal Firefighters Museum

There were no fire stations in Montreal before 1852. The first fire hydrants plugged into water pipes appeared in 1863. A fire pump in 1905 required four people to operate it. Horses were formally retired from service in 1936 and a fireman carries 30 lbs of equipment when working.

The Montreal Firefighters Museum, at the corner of Laurier and St-Laurent, is housed in the beautiful former City Hall of the town of St-Louis which was annexed by Montreal in 1909. The museum is attached to Fire Station 30, its home since 1980. A couple of hand-detailed antique fire trucks form part of the exhibit; these are loaned out for parades throughout the year.

The museum keeps a detailed listing in thick binders of all Montreal fires. And Montreal, unfortunately, has had some spectacular ones: in 1852 one such fire left 10,000 homeless, about one quarter of the city's population. City Hall was destroyed by fire in 1922.

Before 1981, when a lever located on a fire alarm box located on the street was pulled, that triggered an alarm at headquarters which then transmitted the information to the closest fire station via telex. There were 2,850 alarm boxes in Montreal in the days before 911, one of which is on display, along with all the transmission paraphernalia, in a room dedicated to alarm headquarters.

Auxiliary firemen Barry Adams and Serge Dandurand co-curate the museum. Speeding along to every fire, they also serve sandwiches and coffee from a mobile canteen, provide blankets and other support to firefighters on the job. One room in the museum is dedicated to the exploits of these auxiliary firemen. Tradition is strong with firefighters, which is why the dedication to the job runs in families over generations.

5100 St-Laurent Boulevard
514.872.3757 www.museedespompiers.com (French only)
Métro/Bus: Bus 51 or 55
Hours: Sun., 1:30 p.m.–4 p.m.; closed on holidays
Tours: yes, in French and English; by reservation
Fee: donation appreciated | Gift shop: display case
Cafeteria: no | Wheelchair access: no

A polygraph machine used by the Montreal police, 1950s.

Montreal Police Association Museum

Before 911, the home telephone, and cell phones, there was the police telephone box. Located on street corners throughout Montreal, the painted blue box, usually perched on a utility pole, was the ordinary citizen's way of summoning help.

Before cell phones Montreal Island police officers on duty communicated via walkie-talkie. Since 2001, the 911 dispatch centre has been located in the same building which houses the Montreal Police Association Museum—a large, white edifice across from Place-des-Arts.

Exhibits feature the history of Montreal police uniforms. In 1963 the outfit resembled an RCMP officer's, complete with jodhpurs, zipped up boots and cap over one eye. Leather caps and aviator glasses in the style of the Red Baron, a mannequin on a reconstructed red police motorcycle, and a wall of honour commemorating the men and women who died in the line of duty are a sombre reminder of the dangers that members of the 5,000-strong force, thirty per cent of whom are women, face daily.

The permanent collection, in the same room where press conferences are held, conveys a taste of police life. Of note are the enormous shiny prison cell keys and the indestructible 1950s polygraph. The main exhibit is displayed on the ground floor, but interesting historical objects and photographs are found throughout the building, including a highly-polished nineteenth-century Montreal Police silver ceremonial sword and scabbard, a giant Rolodex of every street in Montreal, and an equally large telex machine that connected to individual police stations.

1441 St-Urbain Street, ground floor
514.280.2043 ww.spvm.qc.ca
Métro/Bus: Place-des-Arts
Hours: Tuesdays and Thursdays, 9 a.m.-noon; by appointment
Tours: Only guided tours; specify French or English; 1-50 people
Fee: free | Gift shop: display case | Cafeteria: no
Wheelchair accessible: yes

The castle-like main entrance to the Les Fusiliers' armoury.

Museum of Les Fusiliers Mont-Royal

An impressive sight greets you at the Museum of Les Fusiliers Mont-Royal: a striking chandelier created from swords, and a lamp made of bayonets. These fixtures fit in perfectly with the polished military atmosphere of Canada's oldest French militia battalion, the regiment that was founded in 1869 as the 65th Batallion which became the Carabiniers Mount Royal in 1902.

The armoury, designed as a castle with four round towers, was built in 1910, and takes up most of a city block on the Plateau. It is now a national historic site. Les Fusiliers Mont-Royal's motto is *Nunquam retrosorum*—Never retreat. Red, black, white, and gold are the elegant regimental colours, and they weave their way through the officers' mess, the card room, and the museum, which was founded in 1977.

Among the more curious objects on display is a pamphlet on Icelandic for Soldiers—the Fusiliers served in Iceland during World War II, and Brigadier J.G. Gauvreau returned years later to serve as Canadian Ambassador to Iceland. The first flag of Québec with gold metal fringes, is elegantly draped in a glass case, fleur-de-lis proudly on display. A collection of captains' caps, metal helmets, pillbox hats and the ever-present bugle presents another aspect of the regiment's history. A portable telegraph from 1917 was the height of communication during World War I.

A list of the battles in which the Fusiliers fought, from Butte to Dieppe, and a replica of the Dieppe monument dedicated to Canadians, forms part of the collection. A treasure trove of badges and medals, arranged by rank and encased in pull-out shelving, is an enthusiast's delight; a complete soldier's field kit gives a taste of the sparse realities of a soldier's life.

3721 Henri-Julien Avenue
514.283.7444, x. 230 www.lesfusiliersmont-royal.com
Métro/Bus: Sherbrooke; Bus144
Hours: by appointment only, Mon.-Fri. 9 a.m.-4 p.m.;
 Tues. 6:30 p.m.-9 p.m.
Tours: yes, by appointment only | Fee: free |
Gift shop: display case | Cafeteria: no | Wheelchair access: partial

Life-size mannquins convey the mission of the
Sisters of Miséricordia.

Museum of the Miséricordia Sisters

It is a peaceful place, located along the meandering Rivière-des-Prairies, surrounded by manicured green lawns graced by hundred-year-old trees. The Motherhouse of the Sisters of Misericordia has a long history serving the community of Montreal.

A midwife by training, Sister Rosalie Cadron-Jetté, the founder of the order more than 150 years ago, was the mother of 11 children. Widowed young, she took upon herself the daunting task of caring for unwed mothers and their unwanted babies at a time when both were shunned by society.

Particularly touching, in the museum, are the many black-and-white photographs of the children in their care. Nurseries took care of babies until three years of age; a school operated between 1943-1951, to provide the children with a sense of normal life. Homes for unwed mothers were established so that the mostly teenaged girls could be taught skills to enable them to earn a living. The order also constructed the Miséricordia Hospital with a focus on pediatrics and obstetrics; its graystone building now functions as the CHSLD Jacques-Viger on René-Levésque Boulevard.

The few objects owned by Sister Rosalie, such as her rosaries and a few eating utensils, convey a sense of the simple life she lived.

From those humble beginnings, Sister Rosalie, who took the name Sister Nativity, is on her way to being canonized. Her concept of caring with love and compassion for unwed mothers has spread to missions in Ecuador, Cameroon, and the United States.

12435 avenue de la Miséricorde, Cartierville
514.332-0550, x. 393 www.smisericorde.org/Amusee.htm
Métro/Bus: Cote-Vertu, then bus 64 north, then walk
Hours: by appointment only
Tours: guided only, by reservation; up to 30 people
Fee: free | Gift shop: yes | Cafeteria: no
Wheelchair access: yes

(top) The museum is housed in the Lovell building. Lovell Litho was the oldest family-owned printing company in Canada.
(bottom) Drawers containing individual letters of lead type.

Printing Museum of Québec

Tucked away on an out-of-the-way street in Old Montreal is a printer and graphic artist's delight—the Printing Museum of Québec located on three floors of a substantial brick building with wooden floors and newel-posted staircases.

Museum founder and retired psychologist Michel Desjardins conceived the idea of a printing museum in 1982, when printing presses in Montreal were giving way to computers. Opened in 2007, the museum blends well with its environment, the five-storey Lovell Litho & Publications building, rebuilt in 1885 on the ashes and site of the 1835 edifice. The importance of freedom of speech, and its dissemination through the printed word, is at the core of the museum's raison d'être.

Here you enter the world of linotype machines, wood-cut letters, and drawers full of vintage lead type. Some of the multi-ton machines of that era are the centrepieces of the museum: a massive linotype machine with a melting pot for the metal type, a monotype machine, a hot-stamp press which produces gold-foil decorative symbols, and a binding machine—the only machine which women were permitted to use.

Printer Nelson Tousignant, who began in the business in 1955, delights in showing visitors how to print their names using woodblocks and a giant metal roller. The museum is run by enthusiastic volunteers who want to share their knowledge with you. There are annual seminars on printing and freedom of speech by professors and other experts, and classes on printing for students and the general public. Colourful posters printed by students using the museum's presses are available in the small boutique.

423 Saint-Nicolas Street, Old Montreal
514.971.3800 www.museeimpression.org
Métro: Square Victoria; Place-d'Armes
Hours: flexible; by appointment only
Tours: 1-25 people; in English and French
Fee: $9; $6 (students) | Gift shop: display case
Cafeteria: no | Wheelchair access: partial

The Québec Rock 'n' Roll Museum is jam-packed with lively mementos of that rocking era.

Québec Rock 'n'Roll Museum

You've danced the Bop and done the Stroll
The Conga-rock is getting old
Now clap your hands right through the dance
The beat will put you in a trance
Clap your hands, clap your hands

That 1950s hit by the *Beau-Marks*, formerly the *Del-tones*, reached #45 on Billboard charts and #1 in Canada. The *Beau-Marks* were a Québec band, one of several with hit songs in the U.S. The Québec Rock'n'Roll Museum, a large jam-packed room, is filled with facts of the world-changing genre and its influence on Québec, and how, in turn, the province's rock'n'roll artists influenced the world.

Québec has a well-known love affair with Elvis Presley. Patrice Caron, the museum's sole employee, a fund of fascinating facts on Québec's Golden Age of Music, believes that the connection can be traced to the Quiet Revolution and throwing off the shackles of the Catholic Church in the early 1960s.

The walls are plastered with posters of the cream of Québec rock'n'roll: producer Roger Miron, teen idol Billy Mason, singer Carmen Déziel, *Les Mégatones*, and the *T-Birds*. The original drum used by the *Beau-Marks*, donated by the family, sits beside a working 1962 jukebox.

The building, a shoe factory in the 1930s, morphed into an amplifier workshop, renting space on the side for up-and-coming bands. All floors are now dedicated to music: a studio used by the Francofolies and the Montreal Jazz Festival, a post-production studio, a music store, spaces for conferences, speakers, and late-night parties celebrating Québec music.

Rock on!

2222 Ontario Street East, Suite 314
514.225-4127 www.museedurocknrollduquebec.com
Métro: Frontenac, then bus 125 west
Hours: by appointment
Tours: yes, in French and English; reservations required
Fee: donation | Gift shop: display stand | Cafeteria: no
Wheelchair access: no

These instruments that Nobel laureate Sir Ernest Rutherford actually used at McGill (1898-1907) are part of the history of physics.

Rutherford Museum

Like a late 1800s physics lab, the Rutherford Museum is filled with odd-looking tools of entwined wires and tubes, all encased in glass and wood display cases.

The Rutherford Museum, an important part of physics history, is a repository of scientific treasures, important not only for their rarity, but because they are the actual instruments Nobel laureate Sir Ernest Rutherford worked with during his nine-year residency at McGill University (1898-1907). Together with Frederick Soddy, New Zealand-born Rutherford conceived of, and wrote the nine papers that established the laws of radioactivity while he was at McGill. They garnered him the joint Nobel Prize in Physics in 1908.

Professor Emeritus Jean Barrette curates the museum. A former McGill physics professor, the museum is his labour of love. He points out each of the instruments made by Sir Ernest, including a quadrantelectrometer, an alphameter, and a gold-leaf electroscope, used to measure miniscule amounts of radiation. Before the dangers of radiation were understood, scientists worked in the lab in three-piece suits, ties, and lab coats. No gloves, no special protection.

One book in the museum's collection is inscribed by Rutherford and a handwritten curriculum vitae in the scientist's hand is another rarity, as are 60 of the papers he wrote while professor of experimental physics. New Zealand honoured its native son by depicting him on its $100 bill. Another point of pride is the heavy wood desk that Rutherford used in his home in Montreal, on and under which are letters and other ephemera. Rutherford's spirit lives on in the room!

McGill University, Rutherford Physics Building, 3600 University, Room 110
514.398.7030 www.physics.mcgill.ca/museum/apparatus.htm
Métro/Bus: McGill; Bus 24
Hours: Mon.-Fri. by appointment; closed during Christmas
　　holidays
Tours: yes, by reservation | Fee: free | Gift shop: no
Cafeteria: no | Wheelchair access: partial

The archives house rare and unusual books dating
from the 16th century.

Sir William Osler Medical Archives

Sir William Osler, considered by some to be the Father of Modern Medicine, is still present in the medical archives named after him—his ashes rest beneath his elegant bust located at the far end of the archives on the third floor of the McIntyre Medical Sciences Building, up the hill at the crown of McGill University.

Sir William instituted the system of medical residency and was instrumental in the founding of Johns Hopkins Hospital and the Johns Hopkins University School of Medicine in Baltimore.

Archivist Chris Lyons has been the keeper of the records for several years, with the dual mission of promoting Oslerian medicine and having "people understand their history".

The archives, designed by renowned architect Percy Knobbs, is furnished with carpets from 1929, oak furnishings, and an air of 19th-century elegance. Eight thousand books on medicine are stacked on its shelves. Two to three exhibits are curated annually.

The archives house rare and unusual books such as an anatomical text, circa 1543, now worth $500,000, donated by Sir William; a 1640 edition of *Religious Medicine* by Thomas Browne, an obstetrical atlas circa 1761 donated by a McGill graduate; a 1759 edition of *Exposition Anatomique* by Jacques Gautier d'Agoty and a book inscribed by Florence Nightingale and found by Lyons. The oldest item in the collection is a valued 2,700-year-old Sumerian cuneiform tablet on ophthalmology.

The archives are open to students and visitors, many of whom come from as far away as Japan and New Zealand.

3655 Promenade Sir-William-Osler, (just south of avenue des Pins, **3rd floor**
514.398.4475, ext. 09873 http://osler.library.mcgill.ca/archives
Metro/Bus: Peel, Bus107 or bus 144
Hours: Mon.-Fri., 9 a.m.-5 p.m.; summers Mon.-Thurs.,
9 a.m.-5 p.m.; closed Christmas break and statutory holidays
Tours: self-guided | Fee: free | Gift shop: no | Cafeteria: no
Wheelchair access: yes

A monstrance, with it sunburst design, flanked by candles at the Sisters of Providence Museum.

Sisters of Providence Museum

Humility. Simplicity. Charity.

These three simple words were the guiding principles for Sister Émilie Tavernier Gamélin, the founder of the Community of the Sisters of Providence. Widowed young and left childless by the death of her three young sons, Emilie Gamelin, after much prayer, devoted her life to helping the poor. Msgr Ignace Bourget, Bishop of Montreal, charged her order "to do everything that other congregations don't do."

The Sisters of Providence were the first to offer education for deaf girls in Canada. They called their search for the hidden deaf "the treasure hunt", because in the 1800s being deaf was considered a shameful disability. The sisters had to convince their parents to allow the children to be educated at their Institute for the Deaf. An "Our Father" prayer in sign language is one of the artifacts at the museum, along with audio-phonic amplifiers and books on teaching the deaf. A statue of St. François de Sales, patron saint of deaf children, graces the room. An interesting oddity on display is a series of montages created by nuns made of buttons, clock and watch parts, showing happy children playing and participating in ordinary life. A replica of Mother Émilie's coffin is also on display, along with a giant bell from the Asile de la Providence.

By 1940 the sisters were making 4,000 prison visits, 7,000 visits to the poor, preparing meals for over 600,000 and providing 500,000 free hospital stays. The influence of the Sisters of Providence reached as far west as Oregon, as far east as Egypt, and as far south as Chile and the Philippines; over 7,000 sisters currently belong to the order, making it one of the largest in the world.

12055 Grenet Street
514.334.9090 www.providenceintl.org/en/
Métro/Bus: Cote-Vertu, then bus 64 north
Hours: Mon.-Fri., 9 a.m.-5 p.m.; evenings/weekends by reservation only (min. group of five)
Tours: self-guided; tours by reservation (min. groups of five) available in English, French & Spanish
Fee: free | Gift shop: yes | Cafeteria: no | Wheelchair access: yes

Step inside Smith House and discover little-known facts about
Montreal's fabled mountain through interactive displays.

Smith House

Up a winding road on Mount Royal across the road from a corral of sleek black horses of Montreal's Police cavalry sits Smith House, a stone building with a green copper roof, one of the undiscovered treasures of the mountain. Smith House serves as the headquarters for the Friends of the Mountain, the society dedicated to keeping Mount Royal as a nature preserve; it transformed the building into a museum in 1999.

Mount Royal Park, inaugurated in 1876, was designed by the celebrated landscape architect Frederick Law Olmsted in his sole architectural venture outside of the United States. Smith House had been built as the summer getaway of millionaire Hosea B. Smith in the mid-1850s. It has served as an art centre, a police and first-aid station, a hunting and nature museum, and as a park keeper's residence.

Step inside Smith House today and discover little-known facts through interactive displays: Mont-Royal is home to about 180 species of birds, including the barred owl and the Bohemian waxwing. A tramway once ran up the mountain. In 1535 Jacques Cartier named the mountain in honour of King Francis I. Jack-in-the-pulpit and white trillium share the grounds with salamanders and red squirrels. The Prince of Wales (later George V) was fêted at a garden party on the mountain in 1905. Lining the corridors are photographs of formal high society parties, family picnics, Tam-Tam drummers, and skiers. Downstairs, learn about the mountain's geology through actual rocks quarried from it.

A charming restaurant, a gift shop, and an in-house library devoted to the mountain are delightful stopovers for visitors.

1260 Remembrance Road on Mount Royal
514.843.8240 www.themountroyal.qc.ca
Métro/Bus: Mont-Royal, then bus11
Hours: 9 a.m.-5 p.m. daily; closed Christmas Day and New Year
Guided Tours: no | Fee: free | Gift shop: yes | Cafeteria: yes
Wheelchair access: yes (via the back door)

Firemen line up in front of fire station No. 24 in St-Henri, in a photograph that is part of the St-Henri Historical Society's collection.

St-Henri Historical Society

The St-Henri Historical Society has thrived for several decades discreetly wedged beside the art-deco St-Henri Fire Station No. 23. St-Henri borders Atwater to the east, the Turcotte Yards to the west, the Lachine Canal to the south and St-Antoine to the north. It is this district, with its rich history beginning in the late 1600s, that gave birth to both famed strongman Louis St-Cyr and strong Catholic values. Churches dot the area.

Divided into an exhibition hall and a research area, the heart of the society's collection is the 70,000 photographs donated by photographer Adrien Dubuc—a dapper gentleman who recorded the history of the area with his camera and collected any snapshots he could find of the working-class district. The photos give voice to the tough lives, and the joyous moments, of St-Henri's residents.

The most recent exhibition, on children in St-Henri, explored the life of children through the influence of school, church, sports, scouting and family. It describes their lives through photos and objects including toys, hockey gear, a pram, and kids' chairs. An interesting contrast is seen between little girls taking first communion dressed as miniature brides, and the girls in Girl Scout uniforms a few decades later.

Upstairs, the research area, which overlooks the exhibit, is filled with information such as marriage rolls from 1868, editions of *Histoire Québec*, *Nos Racines*, and *La Voix Populaire* dating back decades, and individual photo albums. Atop the library shelves, a Victrola, tools, and vintage toys convey a hint of everyday life in St-Henri.

The exhibits are on from Canadian Thanksgiving to Christmas and resume February to April.

521 Place St-Henri
514.933.1318 www.saint-henri.com
Métro/Bus: St-Henri
Hours: Wed., 5 p.m.-9 p.m.; weekends 11 a.m.-4 p.m.; hours change with exhibit
Tours: self-guided | Fee: free | Gift shop: display case
Cafeteria: no | Wheelchair access: yes (on du Couvent Street)

One of the two remaining stone towers, part of the original
fortifications built by the Sulpicians in 1688.

Stone Towers of St-Sulpice, The

The grey stone towers with the pointed turrets once housed religious sisters who were brought over by the Sulpician order to convert and educate Amerindian girls, many of them lived in the longhouses just beyond the fortifications built by the Parisian-based order of priests. The founder of the order, Jean-Jacques Olier, funded the mission to New France, but never himself crossed the ocean—he'd heard the rumours of how bitterly cold this new continent was.

When visiting the towers, you can catch a glimpse of life as it was on the slopes of Mount Royal three centuries ago through the carefully constructed dioramas. A handful of religious sisters lived in the tower, using the first floor as a kitchen, and the third floor for sleeping quarters. Tiny vertical openings in the walls served to bring in slivers of light, and the ceiling was deliberately low to conserve heat. Residents likely had to keep their heads bent while walking around. The tower is now an open space, with the staircase removed. The second tower, about fifty feet away served as the school for girls; the second floor was an atelier where students could learn useful skills such as sewing. The diorama depicts the large stone oven beside the tower where bread was baked.

A trimmed hedge of greenery now replaces the walled fortifications, adding to the tranquility of the Sulpicians' grounds. Walk around to the back to the first, and largest reflecting pool of its kind in North America—an oasis of calm for the students of the Collège de Montréal housed in the impressive classical U-shaped building where the influence of Louis XIV, the Sun King, is still felt.

2065 Sherbrooke Street West, main entrance
514.935-7775 http://domainedesmessieursdesaintsulpice.com/
Métro/Bus: Guy, or bus 24
Hours: June through August only; Tues.-Fri., 1:00 p.m.
   & 3:00 p.m.; Sat., 10 a.m. & 1 p.m.
Tours: guided only; reservations required for groups
Fee: $7 | Gift shop: no | Cafeteria: no | Wheelchair access: partial

(top) Antique wall phones.
(bottom) Manual and automatic switchboards.

Telecommunications Museum

Forget smart phones and cell phones and think back to when and how it all started. Think of the absolute genius of hearing someone's voice over the miles at a time when letter-writing, the telegraph, and the Pony Express were the norms.

The Telecommunications Museum, a volunteer-run museum created by former Nortel employees, is a place to appreciate the telephone in all its incarnations.

Ken Lyons gives the guided tour at the museum located in a former high school given new life as the Pearson Electrotechnology Centre. Every item on display is functional, from the old-fashioned corded switchboard to the payphone and the Princess phone, a must for every teenage girl in the 1970s. Some phones look like faces, with enormous bells serving as eyes set in a rectangular face; others are bug-eyed with surprise. A heavy, black handset contrasts with the avocado green and harvest gold wall phones and the delicate pale blue Princess phone. Variations of Alexander Graham Bell's 1876 invention, including an explosive atmosphere phone used in mines and flour mills, are displayed throughout the museum.

Lyons is full of phone facts: It took 15-20 men to raise a telephone pole. In the 1920s Canada had 2,657 telephone companies. The Bell Telephone Company came to Canada in 1880. And Alexander Graham Bell went through 400 court cases until the patent for the telephone was awarded to him, as Antonio Meucci had invented a similar telecommunication device around the same time.

A tour of the Telecommunications Museum provides a new appreciation for the tiny, compact cell phone that we use today for communication. The current exhibition, Evolution of Telecommunications, continues until 2015.

5000 René-Huguet, Lachine
514.798.1818, x 1 www.musee-virtuel-virtualmuseum.ca
Métro/Bus: Lionel-Groulx, then bus 496 west
Hours: Mon.-Fri. 10 a.m.–3 p.m.; closed Wed., noon –1 p.m.
Tours: by reservation | Fee: free | Gift shop: no
Cafeteria: no | Wheelchair access: with difficulty

A poster of Donnett the Clown, part of the Jacob-Willem Collection
of circus memorabilia.

TOHU (circus museum)

Montréal is Circus Central, thanks largely to the genius of Guy Laliberté and the Cirque du Soleil. TOHU is the original concept that pulls it together, mixing in the circus arts, community, culture, and environment in a pair of green sustainability buildings located in the St-Michel district.

In the atrium, an animated exhibit of enormous photographs is splashed on the walls, depicting behind-the-scenes at the circus. The Jacob-Willem Collection of circus memorabilia is part of the permanent collection. Set up around the perimeter of the circus ring, surrounded by black velvet curtains, is a selection of artifacts from the 15,000-piece collection. Showcased in glass against brightly-lit red backgrounds, various aspects of circus life come alive in figurines of porcelain, metal, and wood: the clown and his "auguste", the subservient sidekick; the concept of the white clown, costumed in elaborate velvet decorated with sequins and embroidery; the clown's hat, a descendant of the ancient Roman priest's cap; and, of course, the performing cats and geese, lions and horses. As well, the memorabilia from generations of families performing with the Cirque d'hiver de Paris and the aristocratic Cirque Molier, and the foundation of the modern circus by a British cavalry officer in 1768 by the river Thames.

The photography exhibits change every couple of months. Travelling circuses drop in for a week or two, their artists honing their skills before flying off, literally and figuratively for the Big Top.

2345 Jarry Street East
514.376.TOHU (8648) www.tohu.ca/en
Métro/Bus: Iberville, then Bus 94 north; Jarry, then bus 193 east
Hours: every day, 9 a.m.–5 p.m.
Tours: self-guided | Fee: free | Gift shop: yes
Cafeteria: 8 a.m.–11 p.m. during shows; otherwise 8 a.m.–2 p.m.
Wheelchair access: Yes

Neighbourhood Index

Old Montreal

Outremont

(The) Plateau

St-Henri

St-Michel

Westmount

West Island

Subject Index

GONE BUT NOT FORGOTTEN

Doll Museum
Marc-Aurèle Fortin Museum
(collection given to the McCord Museum)
Just for Laughs Museum
Midgets' Palace
Museum of Education
Phonothèque of Montreal
Mariners Museum (now part of the Pointe-à-Callières
Museum)
Museum of Urban Art
Maurice Richard Museum
Notre-Dame Basilica Museum

If you know of any hidden-away Montreal-area museums,
we would love to hear about them.

othermuseums@vehiculepress.com

Photo Credits

p. 2 courtesy of Geoffrey Hall, IRBV; p. 14 - photo, Jean Barrette; p. 16 - courtesy of the Aron Museum; p. 18 - courtesy of the Avmor Collection; p. 20 - photo, Rachelle Alkallay; p. 22 - courtesy of Geoffrey Hall, IRBV; p. 24 - photo, Colin Favret; p. 28 - courtesy of Cal M. Kufta; p. 30 - photos, Robert St-Pierre; p. 32 - courtesy of the Canadian Forces Logistics Museum; p. 34 - courtesy of the Centre des arts contemporains du Québec; p. 36 - courtesy of Eco-Museum Zoo; p. 38 - photo, Carl Lessard; p. 40 - courtesy of Econo-museum of the Violin; p. 42 - photo, Rachelle Alkallay; p. 44 - photo, Rachelle Alkallay; p. 46 - courtesy of André Bérard; p. 48 - credit Maison du développement durable; p. 50 - photo, Susan Moss; p. 52 - courtesy of iMusée: musée de l'informatique du Québec; p. 54 - Maison de Mère d'Youville - photo, Simon Dardick; p. 56 - courtesy of the Montreal Masonic Library/Temple; p. 58 - McGill University Rare Books; p. 60 - Médiathèque Jazz - photo, Simon Dardick; p. 62 - courtesy of the Médiathèque Gaëtan-Dostie; p. 64 - courtesy of Hall of Fame - Canadiens de Montréal; p. 66 - Firefighters - photo, Simon Dardick; p. 68 - courtesy of Musée de la police de Montréal; p. 70 courtesy of Les Fusiliers Mont-Royal; p. 72 - ©michelineleclerc.com; p. 74 - courtesy of Musée de l'imprimerie du Québec; p. 76 - courtesy of Musée du Rock 'n' roll du Québec; p. 78 - courtesy of Jean Barrette; p. 80 - "Reproduced by permission of the Osler Library of the History of Medicine, McGill University"; p. 82 - photo, Rachelle Alkallay; p. 84 - ©Les amis de la montage/Samuel Montigné; p. 86 - Collection: Société historique de Saint-Henri - Cote: 73ph2; p. 88 - photo, Robert Lebeau; p. 90 - photo, Ken Lyons; p. 92 - credit: Fonds Jacob-Willem.